Please return to the branch from which you borrowed on or before the latest date shown below.	
MAR 27 1996	
FEB 1 0 1997	
APR 3 0	
NOV 1 3 1998	
PLEASE LEAVE CARD(S) IN POCKET	

Eating

Anita Ganeri

**RAINTREE
STECK-VAUGHN**
P U B L I S H E R S
The Steck-Vaughn Company

Austin, Texas

Series Editor: Pippa Pollard
Editor: Jane Walker
Science Editor: Kim Merlino
Design: Sally Boothroyd
Project Manager: Julie Klaus
Electronic Production:
   Scott Melcer
Artwork: Cilla Eurich
Cover artwork: Cilla Eurich
Picture Research: Juliet Duff

Library of Congress Cataloging-in-Publication Data
Ganeri, Anita.
   Eating / Anita Ganeri.
      p.   cm. — (First starts)
   Includes index.
   ISBN 0-8114-5522-X
   1. Digestion — Juvenile literature. 2. Ingestion — Juvenile literature. 3. Food habits — Juvenile literature. [1. Digestive system. 2. Digestion.] I. Title. II. Series.
   QP145.G224 1995
   612.3—dc20   94-14375
                                CIP
                                AC

Printed and bound in the United States by Lake Book, Melrose Park, IL

1 2 3 4 5 6 7 8 9 0 LB 98 97 96 95 94

Contents

Why Do You Eat?

Food contains useful substances, called **nutrients**. Your body needs these to help it grow, to repair worn-out parts, and to keep it healthy. Your body also needs energy to make it go, just like a car needs fuel. You get energy from food. You need to eat when your supplies of energy and nutrients run low.

▽ In your lifetime, you and your family will eat about 33 tons (30 tonnes) of food each.

What Is Digestion?

Before your body can use the food you eat, it has to break it down into tiny pieces. These have to be small enough to pass into your blood. Your blood then carries them all around your body. This whole process is called **digestion**. From the minute you take a bite of food, your body begins to digest it.

▽ It usually takes about a day for your body to digest a large meal.

▷ Drinks, soups, and sauces are digested more quickly than solid foods.

▽ It's better if you do not run around after a meal.

The Digestive System

After you swallow your food, you may forget all about it. But your body is busy mixing, mashing, and breaking the food up into tiny pieces. Special chemicals, called **enzymes**, help to break it down. Food travels along a system of tubes and organs while it is being digested. It is a long journey. Your **digestive system** is about 30 feet (9 meters) long.

▽ Your digestive system runs right down your body, from your mouth through your stomach to your rectum.

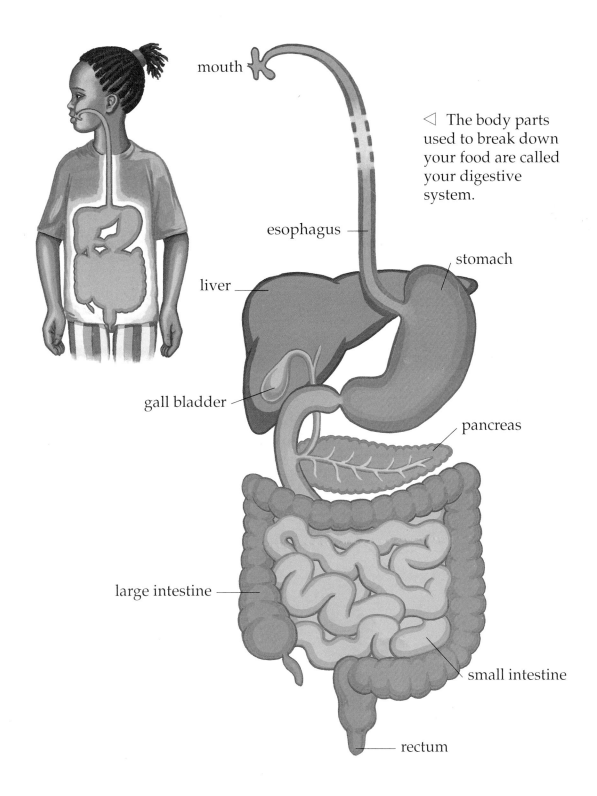

mouth

esophagus

liver

gall bladder

large intestine

stomach

pancreas

small intestine

rectum

◁ The body parts used to break down your food are called your digestive system.

7

Biting and Chewing

The first stop for food is your mouth. Here your teeth bite and chew food into small pieces. As you chew, your mouth makes watery **saliva**, or spit. It wets your food so it is easier to swallow. Saliva also helps to break down and dissolve the food. Your tongue mashes the food and pushes it to the back of your mouth.

▽ There are 32 teeth in a full, adult set of teeth. They grow in place of your first set of teeth, called baby teeth.

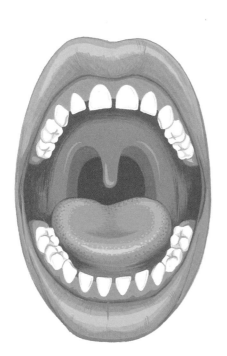

baby teeth

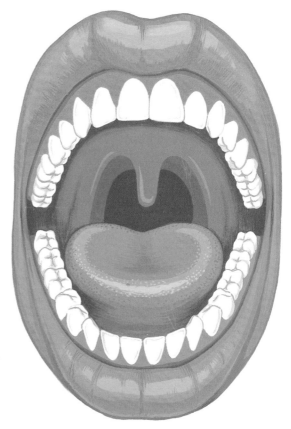

permanent teeth

▷ Saliva is made in special body parts called salivary glands. They lie under your tongue and inside your cheeks.

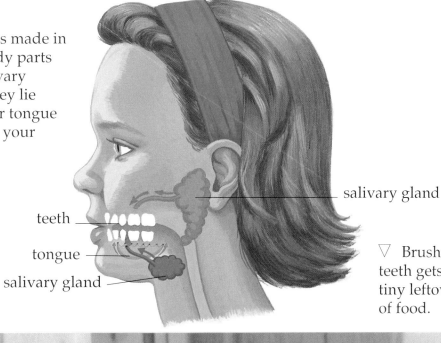

salivary gland

teeth

tongue

salivary gland

▽ Brushing your teeth gets rid of any tiny leftover pieces of food.

Tasting

What is your favorite taste? Do you like sweet things or sharp, sour tasting things? You taste your food with your tongue. It has thousands of tiny bumps on its surface. You can see groups of them if you look at your tongue in the mirror. Between the bumps are cells called **taste buds**. Taste is useful for telling you if something is good or bad to eat.

▽ Your tongue has more than 10,000 taste buds. But they may not work as well when you grow older.

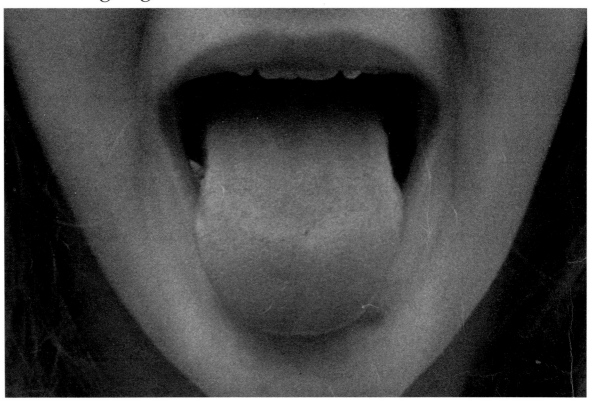

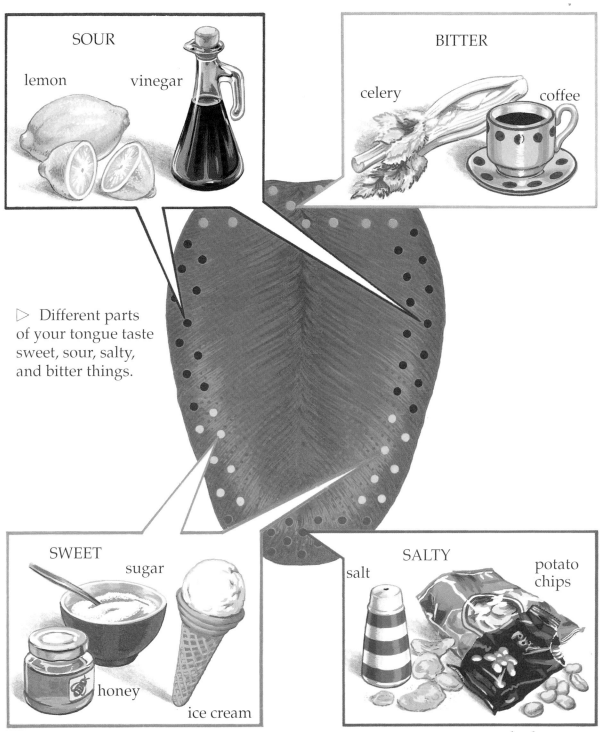

SOUR

lemon

vinegar

BITTER

celery

coffee

▷ Different parts
of your tongue taste
sweet, sour, salty,
and bitter things.

SWEET

sugar

honey

ice cream

SALTY

salt

potato
chips

salted peanuts

Swallowing

When a piece of food is small and soft enough, your tongue pushes it to the back of your mouth. You can then swallow the food. It goes into the first part of your food tube. This is called your **esophagus**. Muscles in the esophagus squeeze together to push the food through. It does not simply slide down.

▷ Muscles in your esophagus squeeze your food in the same way that you squeeze a tube of toothpaste.

▽ A tiny flap, called the epiglottis, stops food from going down your windpipe, or trachea. Sometimes your food goes down the wrong way by mistake.

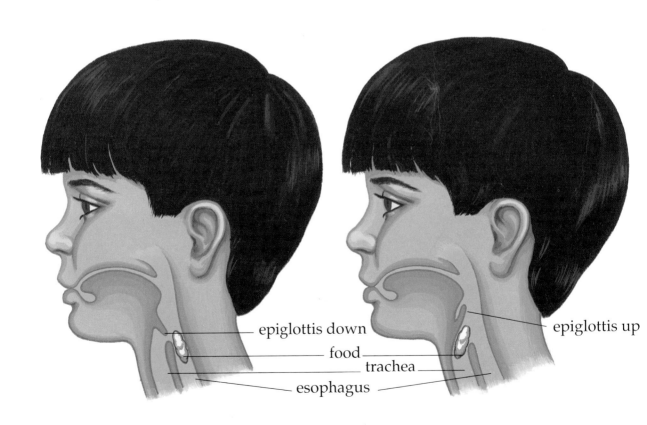

epiglottis down
food
trachea
esophagus
epiglottis up

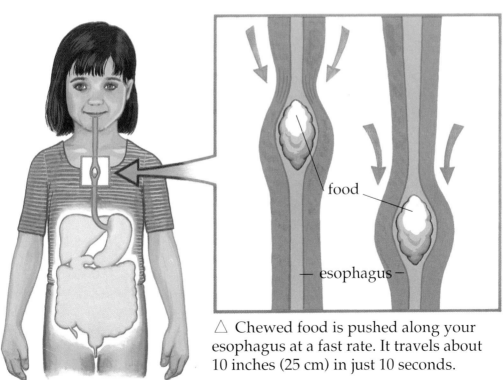

△ Chewed food is pushed along your esophagus at a fast rate. It travels about 10 inches (25 cm) in just 10 seconds.

food

esophagus

Into Your Stomach

Your esophagus leads into your stomach. Your stomach is like a muscular bag that stretches as it fills up with food. In your stomach, your food is squashed and mashed even more. Special digestive juices are poured onto the food. They are a mixture of strong acids and enzymes, and they help to break the food down into simpler substances. The juices also destroy some harmful germs in your food.

▷ Digestive juices are made in the lining of your stomach.

▽ Muscles in the stomach wall help to mix your food and the digestive juices together. Food stays in your stomach for about four hours. By then, it looks like thick soup.

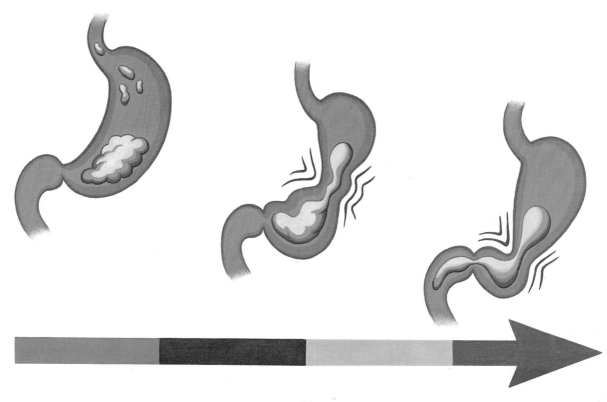

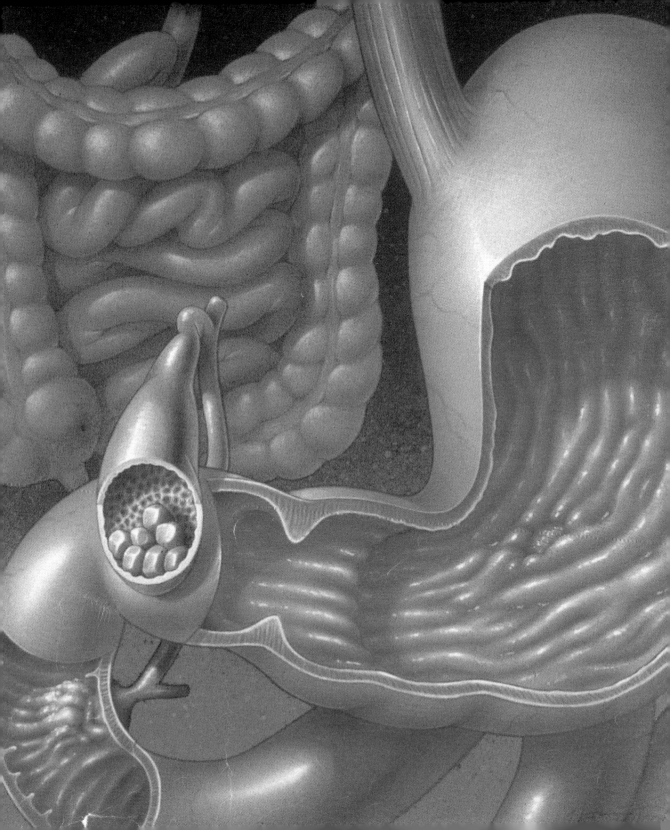

The Small Intestine

From your stomach, your food flows into your **small intestine**. This is a long, narrow tube that is coiled up in the space below your stomach and your liver. In the first part of the tube, more juices pour in from your gall bladder and pancreas. Then the food is ready to seep through the walls of the small intestine and into your blood.

▷ Your small intestine is about three times the length of this jump rope. It is roughly 20 feet (6 meters) long.

▷ Tiny blood vessels inside your small intestine carry digested food into your blood. Much of the food goes to your liver first.

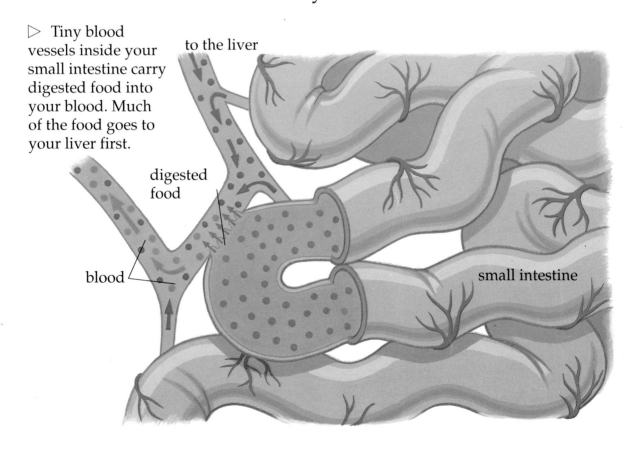

to the liver

digested food

blood

small intestine

The Liver and the Pancreas

Your liver has several important jobs to do in your body. One of these is to make a greenish liquid called **bile**. It helps to break up and digest the fat in your food. The bile is stored in a small bag, called the **gall bladder**. Your **pancreas** also makes juices that break up food as it passes through your small intestine.

▽ This is a model of a human liver with the gall bladder in the middle painted yellow. Your liver is one of the most important organs in your body.

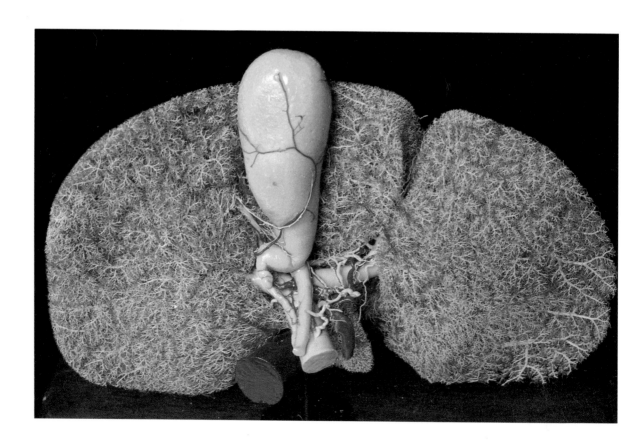

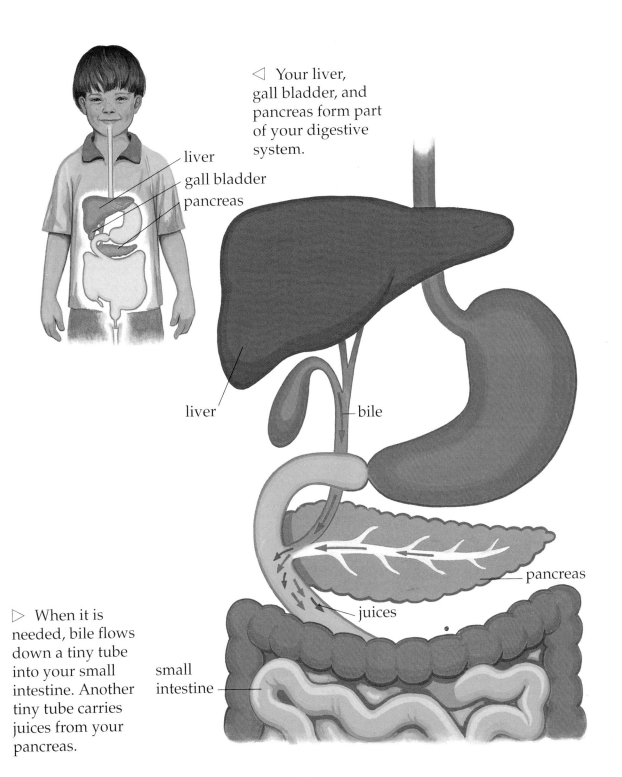

◁ Your liver, gall bladder, and pancreas form part of your digestive system.

liver
gall bladder
pancreas

liver

bile

pancreas

juices

▷ When it is needed, bile flows down a tiny tube into your small intestine. Another tiny tube carries juices from your pancreas.

small intestine

The Large Intestine

Any water and food that have not been digested are pushed into the next tube. This is called your **large intestine**. The useful water passes through the walls of the tube and into your blood. The solid waste food is stored at the end of your large intestine. It finally passes out of your body when you go to the bathroom.

▽ Foods like these help to move food through your digestive system and into your large intestine.

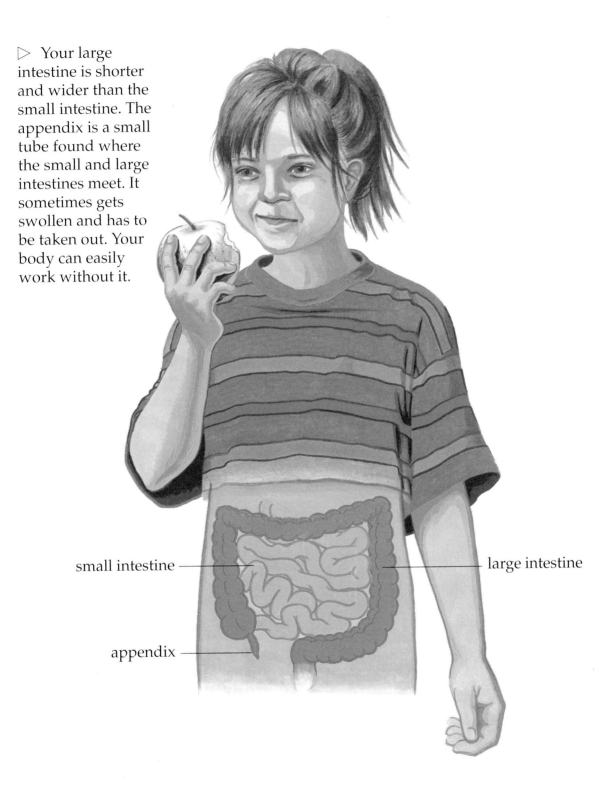

▷ Your large intestine is shorter and wider than the small intestine. The appendix is a small tube found where the small and large intestines meet. It sometimes gets swollen and has to be taken out. Your body can easily work without it.

small intestine

large intestine

appendix

Getting Rid of Waste

Your **kidneys** are not part of your digestive system. But they do help your body to get rid of waste. Your blood flows through your kidneys. They clean the blood and remove any wastes. This process leaves behind a yellowish liquid called urine. It flows into your bladder where it is stored until you urinate.

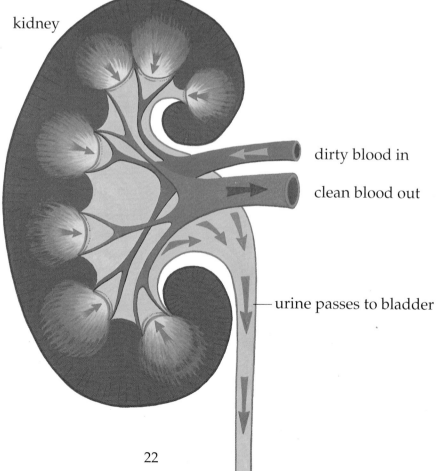

kidney

▷ Dirty blood passes into your kidneys to be cleaned. There are more than a million tiny filters inside each of your kidneys.

dirty blood in

clean blood out

— urine passes to bladder

▷ Your bladder can stretch to hold more urine. The more you drink, the more urine you make.

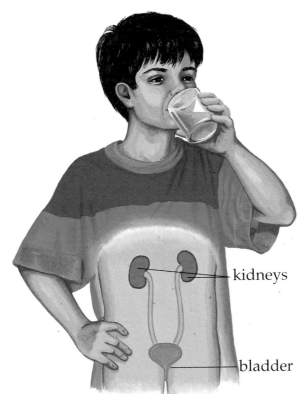

kidneys

bladder

▽ Some people have kidneys that stop working. Their blood has to be cleaned by a special machine called a dialysis machine.

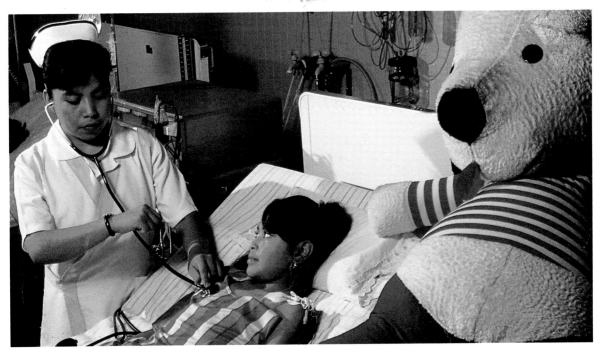

What's in Your Food?

Different types of food contain different nutrients. These do many useful jobs inside your body. They give you energy, help you to grow, and keep your body in good working order. There are five types of nutrients: proteins, carbohydrates, fats, vitamins, and minerals. You need to eat a mixture of these to be healthy. You also need to eat food with **fiber**. It helps your body get rid of waste products.

▷ Fresh fruits and vegetables contain fiber. You will get plenty of fiber if you eat whole grain bread and breakfast cereals.

Fats give you energy and help to keep your red blood cells healthy.

Vitamins and **minerals** keep your body healthy and prevent diseases.

Fiber helps your digestive system work well.

Proteins are used for growth and for body repairs.

Carbohydrates give you energy.

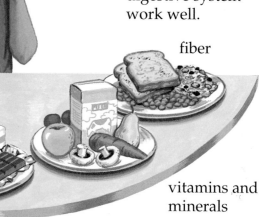

proteins

fiber

fats

vitamins and minerals

carbohydrates

Calories and Exercise

Different types of food contain different amounts of energy. This energy is measured in **kilocalories**, or just calories. Fatty foods contain lots of calories. Sweet or starchy foods contain fewer calories. Salads contain very few. You use many calories when you run or swim. But if you eat too much and don't exercise, you may become overweight and unhealthy.

▽ Exercise helps you to burn off calories and stay in shape and healthy.

▽ Look at the labels on the food you buy. They tell you how many calories and nutrients each food contains.

Nutrition Information		
	per 100 g	per 30 g pack
Energy	533 cal	160 cal
Protein	6.5 g	1.9 g
Carbohydrate	40.1 g	12.0 g
Fat	36.8 g	11.0 g

▷ You burn off up to 600 calories an hour when you swim.

△ You use up as many as 70 calories an hour when you are asleep.

Food Around the World

There is enough food in the world to feed everyone. But it is not shared equally. Often in some poorer countries, especially in Africa, millions of people are starving. Others have some food, but their diet is not varied enough to keep them healthy. In richer countries there is plenty to eat. But some people become ill because they eat too much of the wrong foods.

▷ Millions of people in the world struggle to find enough food to eat.

▷ Fast foods like hamburgers are popular in rich countries. But they often lack some important vitamins, minerals, and fiber.

▷ People around the world rely on a few basic foods, called staples. These foods often grow nearby and form the main part of the local diet.

rice

wheat

root crops

barley

corn

potatoes

millet and
sorghum

Things to Do

- Carry out a survey of foods in the supermarket. Look at labels on the packets. Which foods contain the most proteins or carbohydrates? Make a list of the top five in each food group.

- Saliva makes food easier to chew and swallow. Dry foods are difficult to swallow. Try eating a couple of dry crackers without anything to drink. Then try it with a drink. What is the difference?

Useful Addresses:

Food and Drug Administration
Office of Consumer Affairs
Room 1685
5600 Fishers Lane
Rockville, MD 20857

Society for Nutrition Education
2001 Killebrew Drive
Suite 340
Minneapolis, MN 55425-1882

Glossary

bile A greenish-yellow liquid made in your liver. It helps to break down fatty food.

digestion The way in which your body breaks down food into tiny pieces. They have to be small enough to be able to pass into your blood.

digestive system The parts of your body that break down your food. They include your mouth, stomach, and intestines.

enzyme A special chemical made inside your body. Some enzymes help to break down food.

esophagus The long tube that your food travels down when you swallow. It leads into your stomach.

fiber The tough parts of vegetables, fruit, and whole grain bread. Fiber keeps your digestive system working well.

gall bladder A pouch-like bag, just under your liver, that stores bile.

kidney A part of your body that cleans your blood and makes urine from the wastes. You have two kidneys.

kilocalorie A unit used to measure the amount of energy in food.

large intestine The tube that forms the last part of your digestive system. This is where waste solids are made into feces.

nutrient A substance found in food. Your body uses nutrients for growth and repairs.

pancreas A body part that makes enzymes. They pour from the pancreas into your small intestine.

saliva A watery liquid made in your mouth. It makes food easier to swallow and contains enzymes.

small intestine The long, narrow tube that leads from your stomach. Food seeps from here into your blood.

taste bud A tiny part of your tongue that picks up flavors in your food.

Index

Photographic credits: J. Allan Cash Ltd 26; © Custom Medical Stock Photography 15; Martin Dohrn/ Science Photo Library 20; Chris Fairclough Colour Library 3, 6, 8, 9, 12, 13; Robert Harding Picture Library 5; Anne Kelly/Science Photo Library 10; Frank Spooner Pictures 29; Geoff Tompkinson/ Science Photo Library 23; John Watney Photo Library 18.